THE

TRUTHFULNESS

OF

CHRISTIANITY

DEMONSTRATED AND ILLUSTRATED

IN A SERIES OF

BRIEF ESSAYS.

DEDICATED TO GEN. S. F. CAREY,

The eloquent and successful Advocate of Temperance; and the Friends of Temperance generally,

BY REV. W! ALLINGTON.

CHICAGO:
ADAMS, BLACKMER & LYON,
1866.

NOTE.

—o—

THE following Essays were commenced previous to the war, and have been completed since the writer was relieved from duty as Chaplain in the army, a few months since. Many professed Christians have alleged, as a reason for not identifying themselves with the Temperance cause, the presence of avowed Infidels at the head of Temperance organizations. I have never found their allegations satisfactory, though too much unfaithfulness to Christianity is manifest among many praise worthy friends of abstinence; and too much indifference to Temperance is equally prevalent among many estimable members of the Christian Church. Between Temperance and true religion there can be no antagonism, as the latter includes the former. The author is both a minister of the Gospel and a Temperance advocate, and hopes soon to witness the Church and her handmaid more harmoniously and efficiently engaged in securing the extermination of the greatest obstacle to the honor of God and the happiness of man.

WM. ALLINGTON.

TOLEDO, OHIO, March 24, 1866.

CONTENTS.

"They make the salve a sore, the plaster a plague; they wrist the Scripture to make a wreathe to wrinch their own soule. As they play with the backe of Scripture, so I have turned the edge against them; as they would draw a cloude over the lighte, so I by the beames thereof have chaste away the mist; where they sucke poyson, we finde pearles; wherewith they would wounde even with error, we wind ourselves out of their snares. If any man thinke this labour superfluous, and that our faithe ought not to be drawne to questions, and that controversies breede rather contention than contentment, and tend rather to division than tender edefying; and that consent in faithe is better than contention about faith, and unitie to be preferred before varietie; I answere, healthe is better than wounds, and soundness than sickness; yet the bodie, when it is wounded must be healed; so error when it is spread must be dispersed, and heresie set on foote must be confuted, and poyson infecting must be kept from festering. Peace is to be embraced, but where the truth is not defaced; unitie is to be desired, but where the veritie is not defeated; and love to be maintained, where religion is not impugned."

BRIEF ESSAYS

ON THE

TRUTH OF CHRISTIANITY.

INTRODUCTION.

IN consequence of the prevalence of skepticism in some of its multifarious forms and manifestations among many of our members of Temperance institutions, and the consequent repudiation of membership therein by numbers of professing Christians, I have been influenced to write a series of brief essays illustrative and confirmatory of the Christian religion. In approaching you, reader, as the advocate of a pure and simple faith, I shall not attempt to captivate your imagination by the charms of novelty, nor tax your patience by elaborate explanations. The reasons I shall adduce in support of piety are already hoary with antiquity. More modern evidence, if available, is neither essential nor expedient. Profound logic, an extensive literature, and deep skill in metaphysics are not so necessary to constitute us capable of accurately judging in matters of spiritual experience, as an honest heart and humble disposition; not the arrogant, but modest enquirer, makes real progress in the discovery and practice of divine truth. We realize no timidity in confronting our opponents on the fair field of disputation. We approach fearlessly the test of both history and criticism, ethics, and metaphysics, declining the use of no honorable weapon, and desiring no triumph which may be attributed "to the pointed shafts of ridicule, or to the poisonous arts of insinuation."

FOES AND FRIENDS OF CHRISTIANITY.

Christianity from its original establishment has never lacked opponents, among whom are enumerated, Voltaire, Herbert, Hume, Bolingbroke, Diderot, Toland, Tindal, Chubb, Hobbes, Shaftesbury, Gibbon, Paine, Woolstone, Wharton, Rousseau and a multitude of subordinates, who having vainly attempted the subversion of the Christian religion, died disappointed men. Christianity has also been blessed with advocates and defenders, as Clemens Romans, Ignatius, Polycarp, Justin Martyr, Irenæus, Tatian, Athenagoras, Theophilus, Antiochenus, and others living in the early portion of the Christian era, and Locke, Malbrauche, Berkeley, Taylor, Cudworth, Boyle, Wilkins, Barrow, Clarke, Newton and others of more modern times, but of equally deserved celebrity.

Infidelity, we concede, has had its zealots, and errors of the most malignant tendency have been warmly espoused and zealously propagated, while their advocates have reproached piety as a priestly invention, and have boasted of the freedom and openness with which they oppose the peculiar and distinguishing doctrines of revelation. A caviling mind objects to the plainest truths. Some reprobate certain truths because others approbate them. They are devotees to singularity and rail at truth as the youthful Athenians did against Alcibiades, because the worthy applauded him. Whatever flatters their vanity or pampers their inclination is pronounced honorable; whatever frowns on their passions and abridges their deleterious freedom is calumniated as false. Truths flashing conviction and captivating reason, when understood, they oppose, and stigmatize with fallacy, though too self-evident to necessitate proof. A proposition more transparent and convincing than "The same thing cannot both be and not be at the same time" cannot be framed; yet according to Aristotle, some philosophers denied it. Zeno would not admit motion, and Berkeley denied the existence of the material world except to the mind that perceived it. A man can be a Christian when not a commentator, or an adept at ancient Jewish and Gentile customs. There may be difficulty in comparing and computing customs, times, &c., because the Hebrew idioms vary so manifestly from ours. But these difficulties should never be deemed sufficient to overthrow the faith, because a knowledge of them is not essential to salvation. All pretence to certainty is not to be abandoned even if Christians are not capable of replying satisfactorily to the enquiries of the infidel. A fool may question a philosopher to silence.

IN WHAT CHRISTIANS AND INFIDELS AGREE.

There are grounds which we and skeptics (seem to) occupy in common. We believe

1. In one self-existent, independent God.

2. That he created and still governs the world.

3. That he is impeccable though suffering the existence of evil, both natural and moral.

4. That he is worthy of, and should receive, rational worship.

5. That he desires and promotes human happiness.

6. That he commands and accepts human repentance.

7. That hereafter are rewards and punishments for man.

8. That the New Testament is the purest and most moral of books.

In *amplifying* these propositions, unbelievers differ among themselves, and, in detail, more still from Christian writers.

THE PRINCIPAL QUESTIONS

For which we contend in behalf of Revelation are

1. That the Statements of the Scriptures,

[Commands, Promises and Threatenings,] are *matters of fact* and consequently true.

2. That these facts demonstrate the divinity of their author, whom we call God.

THE INFIDEL'S ANSWER.

In reply to the above two propositions, they say

1. The antiquity of the Scriptures prevents our ascertaining with correctness, the fact of their truth.

2. That when they were originally promulgated, probably no one lived capâble of detecting their falsehood.

3. That previous to the invention of printing, deception was easily and frequently practiced on the unwary.

4. That we are ignorant of many of the false religions which have been imposed pompously upon mankind.

5. That the testimony of the Apostles is disallowed because of their manifest partiality.

6. That the non-fulfillment of promises and prophecies in Scripture, the obscurity and contradiction of its statements, warrant us to suspect its truth.

7. That there is, therefore, good and valid reason to doubt the sincerity and accuracy of Bible writers.

These are the *principal* objections of Infidels to the Bible.

OUR REPLY

Will be embodied in three general propositions, discussed and elaborated in short and distinct chapters, containing the following thoughts:

First, That matters of fact, though long since occurring, may have sufficient evidence to render man culpable, should he refuse to believe.

Second, That the teachings of the New Testament are in themselves beyond all suspicion.

Third, That the testimony given by the Apostles of their sincerity is satisfactory, and that therefore they should be believed.

SEEK TRUTH CALMLY

This controversy must not be considered a trial of wit, my reader, as that might influence us to deem it less honorable to acknowledge an error, than to defend it contrary to evidence, and thus the question would be, not who exhibits the most reason, but the most passion. Truth, like pearls, is found only in a calm. When a disputant is defeated, and yet refuses to surrender, with evidence weak and obstinacy strong, bluster and vehemence are called to his assistance, the miserable supports of a sinking cause. Men, when lacking arguments to relieve a drooping proposition, frequently supply the necessity with noise and clamor. As a gentle rain enters the earth, so truth the ears, and is received by the intellect and the heart.

REJECTION—WHAT IT INVOLVES.

Skeptics professedly refuse subscription to the statements of Revelation by reason of difficulties therein contained, both irreconcilable and insurmountable to reason, whose removal would pave the way to their conversion; though they obstinately object to sacrifice their crude notions and precarious opinions respecting truth, to the peace of the world, established by the reception of the religion of Christ. It is too evident for controversy, that infidel errors, if successfully advocated, would annihilate all hope pointing to immortality, loosen the best cement of society, and overturn the foundations of all religion both natural and revealed. In consequence of pious frauds practiced by some religious instructors, they contend it is impossible to ascertain satisfactorily whether the New Testament revelations are authentic or fictitious. Atheists have advanced against all religions objections of kindred character;

they are without force respecting the Divine existence, and equally vulnerable against the Christian faith; the common consent of mankind overcomes the one, the testimony of mankind destroys the other. No testimony guaranteeing the authenticity of any book equals the evidence demonstrating the truthfulness of revelation. The writings of Greek and Latin historians are but seldom questioned, though one of the greatest proofs adduced to substantiate their correctness, is the writer's testimony. The objections of Infidels are against those histories. How know we the magnitude and splendor of the Roman Empire, delivered by her own interested children? Can we disprove that Catiline was of unimpeachable integrity? that Carthage demolished Rome? that Hannibal overthrew the Roman Empire? May not histories have been written, though now in oblivion, disproving all we believe of these things? How know we that the Macedonians destroyed the

Persians? The accounts of Alexander's celebrated expedition were penned by Gre cians. Not one thousandth portion of the fidelity evinced by the Apostles was manifest in these writers. What estimate would be formed of him, questioning the veracity of our histories because written by our own countrymen? Infidels must repudiate all testimony. We should never countenance unreasoning credulity, nor sanction excessive distrust and suspicion. The prudent character will weigh arguments, consider objections, and decide in harmony with evidence. Deception is possible, but not necessary. The marrow of the skeptic's argument is, because my companion is sufficiently base to take ad vantage of my credulous and confiding heart, I should withhold confidence from all. Because frauds *have been*, it is contended that Christianity may *be* another.

HUMAN SOCIETY.

Society among men is established on the supposition of mutual confidence, but in controversy with Infidels we find every principle of this nature is doubted, if not absolutely destroyed. The integrity of some individuals is so manifest and meritorious, that on them others venture their lives. Characters of the greatest prudence and sagacity have reposed in confidence on the moral honesty of others. What affairs of importance could be transacted apart from this? Men unceasingly confide in each other in the discharge and performance of their various mutual obligations. Why live in perpetual alarm because of the *possibility* of deception? If this be considered unreasonable, then the very legitimate and justifiable inference is, that in some men we may confide, notwithstanding the possibility of deception.

WHEN AND WHY SHOULD MEN BELIEVE.

We now enquire respecting that assurance which influences man to trust. Never should one be induced to believe simply because urged or advised. Either the reputation of a man's purity among individuals of prudence and discernment, or protracted observation and experience of him ourselves, may justify our reposing confidence in him. Now a man's testimony can be transmitted to us by persons of acknowledged probity and intelligence, through a series of centuries, as accurately and as satisfactorily, as a distance of a hundred miles in writing. The principal object to be ascertained would be, whether the matters received were by their reputed authors, and if so, are they deserving of credit. We might illustrate our meaning by showing *how to ascertain the truthfulness of a secular work.* Josephus is reported to have written a book on the Antiquity and Wars of the Jews. We hear he possessed an inquisitive mind, existed in the age of those occurrences he relates, was intimately acquainted with their origin, progress, and termination. Satisfied thus far, we enquire further—Does he merit our confidence? We then receive information respecting the admiration of his history by the learned of the day. But multitudes of fictitious histories are extant—how demonstrate Josephus the author of this? Then we hear the decisions of those competent to judge, examine the history, its style—the character of the historian—compare his narrations with the acknowledged histories of that date, and eventually conclude Josephus the writer. That unauthenticated histories are in circulation is indisputable, but does this evince the impossibility of others being genuine? Because a counterfeit Berosus, Manetho and Philo are read, have we no genuine Strabo or Herodotus? Should the acknowledged fact of the Alexandrian war connected with

Cæsar's commentaries having been written by an individual unknown, invalidate the authenticity of Cæsar's work? Why should we suspect the entire works of Cicero because some one wrote a book assuming the orator's name? Notwithstanding, then, the distance of time since certain events are said to have occurred, and the circulation of spurious publications relative thereto, we may be certain from the testimony offered by adequate authority of which we are judges, both of the fidelity of the men, and the genuineness of their work.

THE AMOUNT OF EVIDENCE NEEDED.

We concede unceasingly, in multiplied instances, that there is sufficient reason for acknowledging the truthfulness of statements made thousands of years since, and conveyed to us as are the matters of fact reported in Scripture. It is but reasonable we should give an assent, as intelligent and strong to the history of the Gospel that we would to "Livy," Thales, Pythagoras or any other ancient writer. The obligation to believe depends on the character and amount of evidence.

AN OBJECTION

Is often urged thus—The facts of Scripture pretend to be of such a miraculous nature, having never fallen beneath our personal inspection, and urging such unprecedented demands on the confidence and affection of humanity, that they are not to be credited, though urged by evidence the most unexceptionable the understanding could appreciate. The strength of this objection is here,—nothing should be the object of belief which is contrary to our uniform experience. Upon this principle, events plainly deducible from the constitution of nature, and easily accounted for upon mechanical principles, will be excluded from credit as much as Christianity. Acting in harmony with this idea, the inhabitants of the Torrid Zone will refuse to believe that water frequently becomes as solid as stone itself. It is to fundamentally destroy all use of human testimony, to refuse confidence to multitudes of witnesses; except by arguments other than theirs, we had been previously convinced of the truth of their allegations. We are always permitted to demand such a degree of evidence as is fully proportionate to the natural incredibility of the event to be attested; and, having received it, to refuse subsequently our acknowledgment of the existence of the fact in whose support it is urged, is obviously repugnant to the sentiments and practices of mankind.

MIRACLES AND MIRACULOUS FACTS.

The facts of Scripture, designated miraculous, are capable of being demonstrated by testimony, though having never been subjected to our individual investigation. "If miracles may be the objects of sight and evidence, as well as the other more usual facts, no sufficient reason can be assigned, why they should not be the objects of credibility. It is not necessary, therefore, that every individual, who is contemporary with the prophet, and supposed to be interested in the matter of a Divine revelation, should have ocular proof of the prophet's inspiration, because they may be satisfactorily convinced of the truth of this essential point by the united testimony of a sufficient number of living witnesses, into whose competency for judgment, veracity and sincerity, they have abundant opportunity to make the proper inquiry."

TRUTHFULNESS OF MIRACULOUS EVENTS.

An enumeration of those circumstances rendering miraculous facts credible to posterity may more comprehensively elucidate my meaning. A miraculous occurrence should

1. Not be self-contradictory, but in unison with itself.

2. A miracle should be publicly performed.

3. Miracles should be numerous and frequent.

4. They should interest, produce strong impressions, and be examined at the time when wrought.

5. Preserved in history by persons of acknowledged integrity, eye-witnesses of the events they relate, be incapable of being deceived, exhibiting no disposition to deal treacherously with others.

6. No authenticated evidence should be passable that the testimony of the reporters of those events was contradicted, though originally published among enemies invited to an examination of their merit.

7. If their existence were acknowledged by those most interested in demonstrating

them fabulous—and only disputed to what cause they were to be attributed.

8. If the witnesses of those events were numerous, unanimous, of ordinary intelligence, unquestioned veracity, evidencing their sincerity by their works,—by renouncing former antagonistic opinions, foregoing every prospect of earthly honor, and anticipating, as probable, ignominy and persecution, and as a consequence of perseverance, death itself.

9. If those testifiers were enabled to evince the indisputable interposition of superhuman authority in favor of their testimony by the performance of works transcending the unaided capabilities of humanity; and after enduring sufferings the most diabolic and indescribable, cheerfully ascended the martyr's scaffold, and approached the martyr's stake, to attest their unabated attachment to the principles they had espoused.

10. If multitudes of those addressed, of varied countries, professions and dispositions, believed their instructors, and manifested proof of their conversion by an instant dissolution of ancient attachments, and contradicting their former life by proceeding in harmony with the newly received instructions.

11 If the changes since accomplished, both morally and religiously, can with Christian propriety be attributed only to those miraculous facts, and are such as would probably have been upon the supposition of their truthfulness.

12. And, finally, if the severest criticism finds the proof it requires, justifying the opinion that no material article of the evidence of those writings handed us by those witnesses, has experienced alterations, but are as pure and genuine as when originally promulged. If these twelve conditions are complied with in the New Testament, and

we fearlessly allege they are,—then indeed we should more justly merit being accused of indulging unreasonable incredulity, if withholding our assent from them. "In short, where there is the strongest assurance of the existence of any particular series of past facts, which we are capable of acquiring, according to the present frame of our nature, and the state of things in the world, to reject these facts after all, and to pretend to excuse ourselves from not believing them, upon the bare suspicion of a *possibility* that they may be false, is a most manifest contradiction to the principles of common sense, and to the universal practice of mankind."

HUMAN TESTIMONY.

Human testimony has been alleged as a proper medium of belief and practice—that is, human testimony by universal consent, may be so circumstanced as to originate in our minds an assurance or evidence so convincing, that no person of ordinary intelligence would doubt it. Frequently with others' eyes we see, and with their ears we hear, and the testimony of their senses is credited almost as extensively as our own. And who can accuse us of acting unreasonably? That every object demanding the assent of the understanding should be accompanied by the best possible proof, under the circumstances, is all that can be required. To demand more would be rash; to be content with less would be absurd.

OUR SCRIPTURES AND RELIGION SAME AS THE APOSTLES.

But are the Scriptures and Christianity of the nineteenth century the same as were established by Christ, written and propagated by the Apostles? Yes, and a few reasons for our belief may be presented.

1. We prove it from the Scriptures extant in the original languages, and various manu-

scripts and translations of considerable antiquity, some more than sixteen hundred years old.

2. From the acknowledged writings of divines, councils and historians affirming the Scriptures to have been derived from the Apostles, and embodying citations from them.

3. From the fact that the persecution of primitive Christians in their literary productions acknowledge them, though ineffectually attempting their overthrow.

4. From the fact that the histories of numerous nations, the Ethiopic, Persian, Syriac, Sclavonic, and others, assure us that the Scriptures have not only circulated in these countries, but have been translated into their languages.

5. The legislative enactments of persecuting emperors previous to Constantine, and those of the Roman Empire subsequent to his day, testify the same.

6. The universal scattering of the Jews,

who unceasingly acknowledge our Scriptures to have descended from Christ, and the Apostles argue it also.

7. Mahometan nations subscribe sufficiently to our Scriptures to demonstrate the truth of our statements.

8. We prove it from the controversial writings of the friends and foes of the Christian religion. We refer to the names and works of Origen, Athanasius, Eusebius, Cyril, Augustine and others, together with the apologists, Lactantius, Clemens, Alexandrinus, Arnobius, &c.

9. Proof of the existence of Platonists, Peripatetics, &c., is evidence also of their doctrine. Now the records of the Church demonstrate its existence since Apostolic days; its doctrine then, and Scriptures, inevitably follow.

It were easy to enlarge, showing it in perfect harmony with just conceptions of God, that he should commission fallible men to declare his will, and that those to whom such revelations were made, should allege, most positively, their knowledge and approval of the cause they had espoused. Nor is it necessary to enquire whether, on the supposition such persons were employed, if our duty is to believe, for if not, then God must either daily reveal afresh his mind to mankind or make no revelation at all; if so, then are we under as strong an obligation to receive the Apostles' testimony, as were those contemporaneous with the disciples themselves.

WHO ARE THE OPPONENTS OF RELIGION?

Christianity, we concede, has been maligned, but by whom? Its opponents, in a majority of instances, have been characters of manifest incompetency, and have most woefully betrayed their cause by the imbecility of their arguments. A voluptuary devoted to his appetite, a debauchee drowned in sensuality, an ambitious mortal abandoned to schemes of personal aggrandizement, a frivolous, dissipated, empty mind, addicted to the most puerile pursuits buried in his contaminating enjoyments. These have vainly attempted to secure the final overthrow of a superstructure planned in heaven and immovably established on earth. They will no more succeed than will Satan annihilate God's moral government, or pluck the universal scepter from his hand. Such parties are not in a condition maturely to weigh theories requiring depth of thought, have not the capabilities to realize the force of an argument on religion, to compass the Christian system, and embrace the various ramifications of its doctrine.

APPEAL TO THE READER.

When communicating instruction of a religious nature we have frequently to appeal to appetites destitute of ears, to prejudice almost hopelessly blind, to perverseness incapable of attention, to pride invulnerable to entreaty. We become the scoff of the infidel, the butt of the libertine, and are designated enemies to liberty and virtue. But the religion we urge you to embrace, though represented as injurious, far from being destructive of human happiness, if impartially examined, will be seen to have principles conservative, and promotive of joys the most unsullied. Its object is to erect an altar whose foundation shall be consolidated by virtue and justice. From that sacred fane shall truth shed forth its radiance on delighted mortals, whose homage to the Great Parent of the Universe flowing consecutively, shall open to the world increased beauty by rendering universal the belief, that happiness, the true end of human existence, is attainable only by obeying the will, and promoting the honor of God. Is my reader an unbeliever in Revelation, in the Godhead of the Redeemer, in the immortality of the soul, in human responsibility, in an eternity of rewards and punishments? Oh, dismiss your pride, cast off your prejudice; this refuses to perceive the truth, that prevents you from embracing it. Search not for truth as one fearing to find it. Examine in God's name, Revelation for yourselves. Dissect the whole, weigh the principles, measure the inferences. Criticise most freely; not to find fault but truth, not to quarrel with its purity but cordially to embrace it. Bring it to the touchstone before maligning it as counterfeit. Remember the important *difference* between words and arguments. To answer a proposition is not invariably to enervate truth. We hesitate not to say that cold skepticism never benefits its victims whether in the form of Socialism, or Philanterianism by Fourier, and Considerant or Rationalism by Owen, or Individualism by Maccall, or Secularism by Hollyoak, or Decertrationalism by Smith, or

Pantheism by Emerson. You may be inundated by isms and only be the further conducted from truth. Abandon all books, society and associations whose obscenity and contamination, whose fiction and suaviloquy bewitch and endanger but can never sanctify nor save. Do they not unite the siren with the fiend, blunt the moral and intellectual sensibilities, and render hearts increasingly insusceptible to celestial impressions? Implore beyond all things the forgiveness of that dread and Holy Being whose truth is so calumniated. Despair not if unconverted, we reiterate, despair not of regeneration. Remember Newton the enslaved, who became the emancipated, and who celebrated in sweetest strains Jehovah's name in Olney Hymns. Remember Scott, the Socinian, who became the devout Christian and learned instructor, and who cherished towards his once repudiated Redeemer, sentiments of utmost reverence, and gave evidences of diligence the most untiring in the promotion of true religion, and reposed with immovable confidence on his atonement for the world. Remember Wilberforce, the fashionable and gay, "joy and crown of Doncaster races," who from supposing Christian ministers exhibited over zeal in the promulgation of Christian principles and obligation, became the eloquent advocate of a higher toned piety among the aristocracy of his nation. Remember Littleton and West, who, having deliberately and impartially investigated the evidences of Revelation, became converted from Infidelity to Christianity, and who produced two volumes of unanswerable proof vindicatory of those holy truths they had previously reproached. Desire your Maker, through his Son, to dispel those mists which darken the understanding. Oh, that you may so perceive the truth as to embrace it. But if you are an unbeliever and will hear your principles questioned with a resolution not to yield, or dispute purposely to overcome, you will live an Infidel and die a reprobate. Arguments will but harden your heart, evidence inflame your guilt, and defeat highten your obstinacy.

THE TRUTHFULNESS OF THE NEW TESTAMENT.

Unless possessed of some substantial ground for suspicion, human testimony is universally alleged as a sufficient reason for assent. Now if the general grounds of suspicion are applicable to the testimony delivered by the Apostles, the inevitable, and therefore justifiable conclusion is, that they are destitute of claims upon our confidence and affection, and have invalidated their pretensions to integrity. But let us enumerate the legitimate grounds on which suspicion may be based. They are

1. If the advocates of any principles or propositions have in other matters been characterized by cunning or treachery, and are

known as willing to compromise rectitude to secure any terrestrial advantage; or,

2. If the subject advocated be deliberately and dexterously adapted to the vitiated desires of those addressed; or,

3. If the occurrence of the events promulged be attributed to a time and place and circumstances, preventing the possibility of investigating or disproving; or,

4. If the genuine histories of those times demonstrate the story advocated contrary to fact; or,

5. If it, though professedly Divine, be proved contradictory, or unbecoming and unworthy the Divine Majesty—all or any of these grounds renders it obligatory on us to reject it.

FIRST GROUND OF SUSPICION

—If the men advocating any event or principle or theory, &c., are known as crafty, treacherous, &c.

Now, dexterously to practice deception, it

is essential to the actor to be extensively and accurately stratagemical, conversant with the subterfuges of impostors, and versed in both business and men. Politicians and priests are generally regarded as possessed of more than common intelligence, which they are accused of employing superstitiously to arouse the fears and apprehensions of the multitude, and transform religion into a state and political empire by which to control mankind. Now supposing this allegation in substance correct, we enquire—By whom, intending if possible to influence the world to embrace a spurious religion, would fishermen of undisputed indigence, and manifestly destitute of a majority of those qualifications by which the aristocracy as well as the plebeian population are influenced?—By whom, we enquire, would such characters be selected to accomplish their purposes? In consequence of being illiterate they were absolutely incapable of dealing in a manner of polished artifice, even with people of ordinary powers.

Never were men acknowledged to have experienced such progress against hostility of the most deadly description and yet were pronounced simple and unlettered. Their opposers were possessed of both cunning and malice. The Jew was obstinate and the Greek a philosopher, yet both succumbed. To contend the Apostles were impostors is to ignore every day occurrences comprehensible to infantile capacity, is to contend for the superiority of imbecility over power, and ignorance over intelligence. They were either ignorant or the contrary. Wisdom would have prevented them from attempting such a manifest impossibility, the want of it would have eternally rendered their attempts inefficient to secure a conquest over mankind. A man studiously deceptive is obliged to employ art and insinuation; to act the sycophant, to countenance wrong. The Apostles proceeded diametrically opposite to that. They imputed the death of Christ to the murderous disposition of their congregations, refused submission to magisterial authority when forbidden to preach. Deceivers defend deception. The Papists argue for the propriety of rehearsing in the presence of their people the manufactured exploits of their manufactured saints. But where is equivocation or mental reservation among those primitive preachers? They persuaded the people by relating most artlessly plain unvarnished matters of fact. The first thing to be sought in every public functionary is a love for truth. Fraud is incessantly frowned on in the Christian system. If the Apostles acted as do others the purity of whose motives is pronounced unquestionable, they are beyond suspicion.

And what must have been the anticipations of the preachers of Christianity when advocating a system excluding every article of heathen mythology, denying the existence of its gods, and aiming at the absolute destruction of every religious system excepting their own? Can you suppose a design so bold could be attempted and executed with any reasonable expectation of escaping persecution and death? They were exposed to violent bursts of indignation from the unrestrained and encouraged populace—legislation sanctioning the most cruel outrages upon their unprotected persons; the fulminations of enraged magistrates; from interested priests, both among Jews and Gentiles, instigated to intensity at the predicted annihilation and proclaimed inferiority of their respective religious systems. Would men desiring of acting fraudulently mention so artlessly and repeatedly those circumstances, which amongst prejudiced and inconsiderate men, might have rendered both themselves and founder highly obnoxious? What say they of their Master? that his country was despicable, John i. 45, 46; his birth and education mean, Luke ii. 4–7; his life poor,

Matt. xiii. 20; rejected by the rulers, John viii. 48; accused of Sabbath breaking, John v. 16; blasphemy, Matt. ix. 3; reviled as a demoniac, John vii. 28. They exhibit equal candor in acknowledging their own original employments, the scandals of their former lives, their faults and follies after being called by Christ, their unbelief, cowardice, and intemperate zeal. Is this no evidence that in no respect are they solicitous to obtain a reputation meriting the approval of foes, purchased with the loss of their integrity of heart? Their Master was poor and despised, persecuted and murdered, could they rationally hope for affluence and ease and long life, and a friendly pillow on which to die?

Human applause not the motive influencing the Apostles—

It is objected that the Apostles were in circumstances exceedingly low, and therefore the applause of the world seemed a sufficient reward and satisfaction for their sacrifices and sufferings. This to all reflective minds is extremely improbable, if not impossible.

1. All believers were not teachers, nor all applauded who suffered. Women as well as men, the aged as well as the young were the early converts to Christianity.

2. Those who taught concealed themselves behind their Master; and when honor was presented them, titles given, and sacrifices about to be offered, they denied themselves for His glory and honor.

3. If applause had been their aim they were excluded from obtaining other possessions, as their labor was abundant, terrestrial pleasures none, their journeys numerous and protracted, and whole communities their deliberate and persistent enemies.

4. The governors of countries wherever they were, avowedly were unbelievers, the shame and reproach from whom more than counterbalanced the applause received from every friendly source. They were scourged,

imprisoned, persecuted, and pronounced the offscouring of the world.

5. One of the vices against which they most vehemently and incessantly inveighed was that the objection supposes them pursuing. With what depth of sincerity and sadness they reprobated the following of Paul by some, of others Apollos and Cephas? And how unhesitatingly they placed the seal of condemnation on those who ambitiously elevated themselves as leaders of the people, leading them from simplicity and truth.

6. Supposing them to have acted as the objection declares, they must have taught truths as falsehoods, against both knowledge and conscience. We confess it difficult to believe that men will seek human panegyric in preaching known falsehoods, though they are numerous who seek followers and honors in recommending what the multitude believe. The fraud alleged against the Apostles would, we imagine, be detected and exposed by the remorse and repentance of at least

one among the multitudes, whose susceptible conscience would revolt and remonstrate, thus leading to exposure and defeat.

7. They certainly must have been cognizant of the danger into which they were precipitating their souls, thus to violate conscience, and forfeit liberty and life.

8. And that such ambition was the rule of their conduct the holiness of their writings demonstrates impossible. Would they not have united their endeavors to the object they pursued? But the Scriptures, which by inspiration they produce, sanctify and humble, instead of rendering their subjects ambitious and depraved.

SECOND GROUND OF SUSPICION

—If the doctrine advocated be purposely adapted to the corrupt tastes and desires of those addressed.

A tyro in history knows that the conditions of both Jews and Gentiles when Christ and his Apostles established Christianity was such that the religious opinions of the nations harmonized but little with the doctrines of the cross. What principles do you imagine would be asserted and maintained in a religion professedly divine? Might we not most rationally expect the divine existence, the perfections, providence and unity of God, the immutable demarkation existing between good and evil, our obligation to live virtuously, the immortality of the human soul, future rewards and punishments, a power to regenerate the human mind, and the whole calculated to beget in us the profoundest humility, and the most exalted admiration of Jehovah? Do you not, as it were, involuntarily apply those properties to the Christian revelation? From whom then could such a system have proceeded but God? Had the doctrine been of human framing it certainly would have been more philosophically adjusted to the genius and gust of the people. But nothing is more manifest than the contrary. Restraints are placed on man's most prevalent passions. The ambitious, covetous, voluptuous, aye, all descriptions of sinners, are called to the ungrateful practices of mortification, penitence and self-denial.

Their own countrymen demanded a Messiah of pomp and triumph; they represented him under the ignominious character of the crucified. Their nation boasted of their celebrated ritual; they insisted on its perpetual abrogation. Universal conquest was the anticipation of the Jewish heart, the consummation of Jewish ambition. Jerusalem was desired to be the metropolis of universal empire; the Apostles proclaimed the empire of religion the human affections, and legal distinctions separating Jew and Gentile eternally destroyed. False Messiahs were certain of followers, because they assumed a character to which the most rooted hopes and the warmest impressions of the Jews universally inclined. They courted popularity and grasped at dominion, succumbed to the pride of the prince, and fed the superstition of the people, approved the indulgence of the most unhallowed passions, and the most perjured conduct of those whose suffrages they desired to possess. Had the Apostles countenanced the continuance of even the *Mosaic* laws they would have more probably succeeded. But even this they proscribed. So again, if instead of attempting to convert the heathen nations by advocating spiritual truth, they had begun by indulging them in practices repugnant to the precepts of the Gospel, by compromising the differences between the two religions. But they absolutely forbade them to retain the least communication with those favorite idols whom they had previously revered as the founders or benefactors of their respective nations. And yet, notwithstanding this unbending sternness of the Apostles, the obstructions and impediments discouraging the propagation of the Gospel, the incessant opposition from the learning and subtleties of the philosophers, the artifice and influence of the priests, the bigotry and superstition of the illiterate, and without a solitary worldly advantage to recommend it, within thirty years of the pentecostal sermon, vast multitudes of all ranks and conditions were formed into extensive congregations of the faithful and established in almost every flourishing city of the Roman Empire. The despised doctrine therefore of a crucified lawgiver, which prevailed so universally against earthly allurements, the writings of the learned, the persecution of the powerful and the determined hostility of the multitude at large, will be regarded by the unprejudiced and reflecting of mankind, who only are competent judges, as an irrefragable argument "that its original was divine and its protector almighty." Had the Apostles sanctioned the superstition of the Gentiles, their ultimate success would have appeared more probable, but these they charged with idolatry. Had religion been the product of the human intellect, the things most repulsive to carnal reason would have been omitted, but a crucified Christ was the theme on which they most insisted. Our foes can with difficulty imagine it possible that the Christians, if sincere, consistent characters, would have been so ignominiously treated as represented by religious historians. Not only believers but honest and superior heathens were commonly the most reproached and persecuted. Socrates was murdered by perfidious hypocrites, and Plato, in consequence, gave utterance to his thoughts tremblingly. Solon suffered for his beneficence. Demosthenes, Seneca, Cicero, Cato and others were unable by both honesty and learning to save their lives. Have we forgotten Galileo and Raleigh and Jenner and Hervey and the Protestant martyrs of France, Ireland and England itself, Ridley, Cranmer and Latimer?

PROOFS OF THE TRUTHFULNESS OF SCRIPTURE.

Were it necessary I might refer you to both the *internal* and *external* evidences of Christianity. It is evident that the *precepts* of morality cross more on sense, than the *credenda* appear to clash with reason. The sallies of corrupt nature are bridled, and not only actions but desires restrained. Every motion is regulated, mortification inculcated, persecution expected, and self-abnegation taught as obligatory. Pleasures are reserved for the future world. A new system of morality is introduced. Vices deified by sensuality are condemned, and virtues proscribed are canonized. Favor must be returned for injuries, kindness for hatred, and affronts avenged with pardon. Wealth is to be placed in honest poverty, glory in ignominy, ambition in the conquest of heaven. Christianity attacks no man on the weak side, has no maxims fawning on nature and flattering sensuality, permits no crimes, promises no impunity, was propagated by no sword, pressed on the reception of mankind by no fire and devastation, its increase attributed to neither armies nor battles, but has overcome hitherto by suffering, humility and persecution. Was this religion the invention or discovery of man, or the offspring of God?

SCRIPTURES NOT OF HUMAN ORIGIN.

I will briefly submit to your consideration a few reasons for believing the Scriptures not to be the consequences of human cogitation.

1. Because of the integrity of the inspired men as exhibited in their writings.

2. Because of the numerous and weighty obligations they were under to utter truth.

3. Because of the want of motive to such an undertaking.

4. Because of the numbers engaged, of varied countries, ranks and professions, both Pagans and Jews.

5. Because they manifest a complete want of art to successfully conduct an imposture.

6. Because the fact related, if untrue, could not have cheated mankind, as it has, into a belief.

7. Because if an imposture, it is impossible it would have maintained in a day of extensive enlightenment and erudition, such a protracted and increasing credit.

8. Because the writers of Scripture professed inspiration, and confirmed it by a train of facts astounding to its foes.

9. Because of the majesty of Scripture style.

10. Because of the harmony of its multitudinous parts.

11. And the power and efficacy of the doctrines of the Bible on the consciences of men.

This number might be greatly augmented, but enough.

THIRD GROUND OF SUSPICION

—If a refutation of the doctrines advocated be rendered impossible by reason of their being placed at a time and locality unfavorable to search.

There are Christians in the world, and history corroborates the statements of Scripture that Jesus Christ was their founder. This is unquestionable to all who act as men and submit to evidence. This Christ was born in a stable, and passed thirty years in indigence and obscurity. He then commenced the advocacy of a doctrine, which he confirmed with prodigies both unparalleled and unprecedented. Health was imparted to the sick, sight to the blind, life to the dead. Eventually, malice effected his death; his own omnipotence, his resurrection. Twelve men were commissioned to subdue the world to the precepts of the gospel. They obeyed. Success attended their labor, and crowned their endeavors. Religion spread. Libertinism, prejudice and atheism conspired its ruin. Arguments were opposed by philosophers, torments by emperors, and by others the all but omnipotent attractions of sensuality. Christianity multiplied its conquests by disputes, increased by proscription and persecution, and broke through the violence of every opposition. Millions died in the combat, who by the constancy and invincibility of their fortitude demonstrated the truth of their religion, overcome in triumph, though enduring tortures most excessive and of most fiendish ingenuity; and frequently by the disposition they manifested toward their executioners, their calm confidence in Almighty God, and anxious desire that their believing survivors should, if required, follow them to the flames, their murderers became confessors, and their tyrants martyrs

Could reports of these facts, imagine you, be produced upon the world if purely fictitious?

OLD TESTAMENT PREDICTIONS CONCERNING CHRIST.

There are numerous prophecies contained in Old Testament Scriptures relating to important events in the New, sufficient to engage the belief of all seeing their accomplishment. For instance, the particular time when Christ should appear in the world, Gen. xlix. 10, Dan. xix. 26; his being born of a Virgin, Isa. vii. 14; the place of his birth, Micah v. 2; the murder of the infants, Jer. li. 15; the adoration of Christ, Ps. lxxii. 10; his presentation in the Temple, Mal. iii. 1; his flight into Egypt and return, Hos. xi. 2; his way been prepared, Isa. xl. 3; his gentleness, &c., Isa. xlii. 2; his miracles and cures, Isa. xli. 1; his dying for man, Isa. liii.; his betrayel, Ps. cix.; his price, Zech. xi. 12; his entry into Jerusalem, Zech. ix. 9; his being buffeted, &c., Isa. l. 6; his scourging, Isa. lii. 12; vinegar given him, his garments divided, lots cast, Ps. lxix. 21, 22, 18; his resurrection, Ps. xvi. 10; his ascent to heaven, Ps. lxviii. Multitudes of particulars might be given relating to the Messiah revealed in Scripture, some four, some two, some one thousand years previous to the birth of Christ and his Apostles.

WRITINGS OF ANCIENT HEATHENS CONFIRM SCRIPTURE.

In the writings of Zoroaster and Hermes, Trismegistus, his disciple, we find notions expressed of Jesus Christ, styled, "The first begotten Son of God, his dear, immutable, uncorruptible Son, whose name is *ineffable.*" The Greek poets, Orpheus and Hesiod, express themselves to the some purport concerning Christ. These men were before the Apostles.

Again, the prophecies of the *sybils* collected by Lactantius, wherein the life, death, &c., of Jesus Christ are largely described and alleged by Justin Martyn, Origen, Arnobius,

St. Augustine and others, assure us that the doctrines and story of the cross can be no invention of the Apostles. Persons existed at the time and place when these events are declared to have occurred. No religion has been put to a similar trial.

AN OBJECTION NOTICED THAT CHRIST APPEARED AMONG FRIENDS.

It is objected to the truth of Christianity that the Savior appeared among his friends. Supposing it, they evinced their sincerity by demanding and adducing an essential proof of his claims, appealing to time and place and persons and circumstances, declaring their utmost readiness to die rather than deny the truth. If this were fiction why was not some recusant or apostate Jew induced to demonstrate it? Jew or Gentile would have triumphed at the event, and immortalized his name. The objections of our opposers tend to our confirmation.

AN OBJECTION ANSWERED CONCERNING THE DATE OF CHRISTIANITY.

It is objected that Christianity was invented and reduced to a system previous to the existence of Christ, and the unbelieving Volney appears to question the existence of Christ at all. We have precisely the same reasons for expressing ourselves thus concerning those historic personages, Julius Cæsar, Romulus, Augustus, and all history whatsoever.

If it be objected that the opponents of Christianity might have disproved and repudiated its claims at the time it is reported they were presented, though now we are not in possession of the account of it, we reply,

1. Had such a confutation taken place we have neither records nor proof remaining.

2. The facts anciently reported the enemies of religion never pretended to confute, Acts iv. 16.

3. We wrong the Jews, the most virulent antagonists of the primitive Christians, by

supposing such a confutation, and their being incapable of presenting the testimony of those opposers. Heretics of most extraordinary capabilities have pleaded these same Scriptures—Julian, Celsus, Porphyry and others, and never denied their being genuine. The ancient writers of the Church cite the same,—Tertullian, Cyprian, Ignatius, Irenæus, Epiphanius, Hieron and others. They certainly were interested in the truths of Christianity, and were most capable of detecting fraudulent attempts on mankind. "A little before the coming of our Savior there was a general expectation spread all over the Eastern nations, that out of *Judea* should arise a person who should be governor of the whole world, is expressly affirmed by the Roman historians, Luetonius and Tacitus. That there lived in Judea at the time which the Gospel relates, such a person as Jesus of Nazareth, is acknowledged by all authors both Jewish and Pagan, who have written since then. The star that appeared at his birth is mentioned by Chalcidius the Platonist, as is also the journey of the Chaldean Magi. Herod's causing all the children in Bethlehem, under two years old, to be slain, and a reflection made thereupon by the Emperor Augustus, that it was better to be Herod's swine than his son, is related by Macrobius. Many of the miracles which Jesus did, as his healing the lame, the blind, casting out devils, are acknowledged by some of the most implacable enemies of Christianity, by Celsus and Julian, and the authors of the Jewish Talmud. That the power of the heathen gods ceased after the coming of Christ is acknowledged by Porphyry. Many particulars of the collateral history concerning John the Baptist, Herod and Pilate are largely recorded by Josephus; the crucifixion of Christ under Pontius Pilate, is related by Tacitus, and numbers of the most remarkable circumstances attending it, such as the earthquake and miraculous darkness were recorded in the Roman registers, and are in a very particular manner attested by Phlegon."

FOURTH GROUND OF SUSPICION

—*If the Christian story be repugnant to the genuine histories of those times when it was promulged.*

It is a fact that both friends and foes acknowledged those books extant which we now possess, near two thousand years ago—and that the authentic histories of that period, instead of being hostile to Scripture facts, are corroborative of them. I will however dwell briefly on this point. The most considerable Roman historians who flourished at the period when Christianity was reproached, and its advocates persecuted, and whose writings are nearly as ancient as our religion itself, are Tacitus and Luetonius. They are justly confessed as competent testimonies to the point under debate. Tacitus says that in Nero's days (whose reign commenced about twenty years subsequent to the crucifixion) multitudes of Christians resided not only in Judea but also in Rome, against whom persecutions were instituted of such a fiendish character as actually to excite compassion in the very bosom of foes. Luetonius substantiates the assertions of Tacitus. Pliny, the officer of Trajan, in the execution of Christians, writing to that Emperor, says, "that many of both sexes and of every age and rank were infected with this superstition, that it was got into the villages as well as the cities, and that till he had begun to put the laws in execution against them, the temples of the heathen deities were almost deserted, and hardly any one could be found who would buy victims for them." Marcus Antonius, a few years following, says the Christians "were examples of a resolute and obstinate contempt of death." Tacitus, speaking of Christ, says, "He was put to death under Pontius Pilate, who was procurator of Judea in the time of Tiberius." The Jews in some early writings derided Christ as "the man who was hanged." Lucian reproaches Christians for worshiping "a crucified impostor." Porphyry allowed Christ to have been "a wise and pious man, approved by the gods, and taken up into heaven for his distinguished virtues, and yet this Porphyry was a foe. Could our adversaries show that Augustus did not tax the Jews; that Herod never existed; that the Romans were never governors of Judea; that there were neither High Priests nor Pharisees at the period contended for in the New Testament, and those historic quotations above mentioned a forgery, then would they probably succeed in influencing many to believe Christianity fabulous. We conclude then, thus,

1. The greatest opposers of our religion confess Christ to have lived upon the earth.

2. Therefore the whole of Scripture cannot be false.

3. If a portion is acknowledged truthful, of a whole claiming equal truth, then none is untruthful. If any portion is fictitious it must be from either the Apostles or their successors. Not the latter for the reasons presented recently in those quotations, &c., as it is contended by Tacitus that in the days of the Apostles it was established at Rome. Nor by the Apostles for reasons already given.

FIFTH GROUND FOR SUSPICION

—If the doctrine advocated be self contradictory or be proved unbecoming the majesty of God.

We boldly assert the Scriptures to contain or enjoin nothing unworthy the perfections of Jehovah. Study its doctrines; what do you find here? That we are fallen, and are universally corrupt; that repentance and conformity to God's laws are obligatory on us; that our Creator is infinitely compassionate and perfect; that we are redeemed by Christ, and that salvation is consequently possible. The Bible is a distinct and full revelation of all that concerns our duty and happiness. It contains three great branches of religion, referring to God, our neighbor and ourselves. It exceeds infinitely in purity and adaption to man, all the institutes and maxims and aphorisms of ancient and modern philosophers. Study its precepts, they are acknowledged the purest on earth,even by men Satanically attempting to render nugatory their influence. Study its promises of grace and glory. What repugnant to the impeccability of the Almighty is here? Human ornament and oratorical flourishes you will seek in vain. You cannot improve the product of the divine intellect. Plainness is preferred to subtlety. Simplicity is grander than art. How varied the mind by which this hallowed volume was penned, and yet what holy harmony pervades the whole.

AN OBJECTION ANSWERED THAT THE APOSTLES WERE IMPERFECT MEN.

We reply—1. Supposing the objection true, yet how evident and unconcealed their sincerity, how lightly they esteemed human honors, how unwilling to conceal their imperfections, and therefore what confidence and affection their frankness merits, and when they speak favorably of themselves it is ever in self-vindication, and unquestioned.

2. But yielding their infirmities, where are their equals? What magnanimity and self-sacrifice and holy diligence they exhibit. What undaunted firmness, what unquenchable love, what protracted forbearance, what a disposition to forgive, what weeping over sinners, tenderness to the weak. Compare them for virtue with the purest, for loyalty with patriots of most renown, and for disin-

terestedness of spirit with the most justly celebrated of earth's favorite sons—who so worthy of apostolic honors?

ARE NOT MYSTERIES INCOMPATIBLE WITH A DIVINE RELIGION?

If they are nature is no less faulty than revelation, for the unbeliever "cannot survey any field of universal nature, above, beneath, around him, anything animate or inanimate, from the lowly floweret on the heath, to the plants of paradise—from the scantiest insect on the wing to the cherubim and seraphim that worship before the Excellent Glory;—he cannot contemplate his own complete frame" —a spirit immortal dwelling in a tabernacle of clay—without a profound sense of mystery. Can he explain the hidden cause of vegetation, growth and reproduction? Can he explain the agency of the sun, moon and stars; the law of gravitation, binding worlds to worlds by its stupendous power? Can he unfold the various mental phenomena of man's estate; the origin, purpose and prevalence of moral evil; the nature, extent and modifications of creature responsibility? Do not these things, and many others which we cannot enumerate, present to the infidel difficulties, which, *on his own principles*, ought to ensure their rejection from his creed?"

Thus we have examined the grounds of suspicion and found them totally inapplicable to the testimony of the Apostles concerning Christianity.

IGNORANCE AN ENEMY TO HUMAN HAPPINESS.

One grand source of man's infidelity and consequent unhappiness is his ignorance. The pertinacity with which he clings to blind opinions imbibed in infancy, which interweave themselves with his existence, the consequent partiality which warps his mind, prevents its expansion, renders him the slave of fiction and dooms him to perpetual error.

He, too frequently, takes the tone of his ideas on the authority of others, themselves in error, and having an interest in his delusion. This Cimmerian darkness must be removed. It is essential to his happiness. But it exacts more than common exertion. It requires undaunted courage and persevering resolution.

Man must think, and examine for himself, and with impartiality, the opinions presented for his acceptance. Prejudice, too, blessed be God, will meet its downfall. The diffusion of ideas among mankind is no longer superstitiously dreaded. Truths will of necessity be useful. The blustering of Infidels is appearing ridiculous. The smallest reflection makes us to feel the falsity of unbelief. Ignorance and prejudice are both pernicious, but the destiny of both is annihilation. Frequently wickedness has been established by violence, and been made to pass as substantive virtue, but the spread and reception of our holy religion is destroying these inconsistent pretensions, is enabling mankind to judge impartially, to yield conviction, and establish truth upon its own imperishable basis. Because Christianity only can render you happy; embrace it—it is equity—the support of human society—goodness connecting all hearts in indissoluble ties; and gratitude feeding benevolence and nourishing generosity. Diffuse happiness among your circles; with sincerity serve your God, and be assured that the sphere of your actions, enlivened by kindness, illumined by benevolence, will react upon yourselves and render irresistible the conviction that the man securing the honor of God and the happiness of his neighbor, cannot himself be miserable.

We will now endeavor to demonstrate and il lustrate that

The testimony of sincerity, truthfulness, &c., presented by the Apostles was the most satisfactory which could be given, and amply sufficient to render it the duty of man to believe. Conduct of infidels described.

The conclusion though truthful, is nevertheless saddening, that there are but comparatively few persons capable of profound connected meditation. This probably, in some measure, accounts for the swarms of skeptics of comparatively juvenile years. The exercise of intense thought is for the greater number a species of labor as painful as it is seldom. We do not assert that people obliged to labor in order to obtain subsistence, for that reason are incapable of reflection. Then others occupied with gratifying their passions, and employed in procuring themselves pleasures, as rarely think deeply as the positively uninformed. We seldom find unbelievers competent to give a rational opinion of their unbelief. Throughout the world they are more speculative than profound. In the wanderings of their imaginations they with great fatuity believe they have discovered something connected and decisive; and, in consequence, they endeavor to form their theories into a system, which though purely chimerical, they have accustomed themselves to consider as demonstrated and true. They fulminate most unceremoniously, and utter in most indignant language their abhorrence of Christians, and persuade most energetically by pen and tongue their heterodox contemporaries to hasten the overthrow of revealed religion, by widening the existing breach between themselves and it. The idea of dying disappointed and baffled men, in their endeavor to secure the annihilation of what they reproach as priestcraft, and conducting it to a most ignominious death, constantly presents itself to their maddened vision, communicates to their hearts hate and despairing energy, rendering them desperate and daring. They appear determined to obtain possession of the public confidence; and to complete their fiendish purposes assume, most designingly, ingratiating manners, enquire sympathizingly respecting their liberties, urge the propriety of resisting what they pronounce ecclesiastical tyranny, profess to furnish them with a religion, more rational, liberal and pure; undertake, but fail, to expose the alleged arrogance and ignorance of religious instructors, represent the ministers of Christ a multitude of whimsical pretenders; describe themselves as individuals of intelligence; urge the adoption of their system as inevitably productive of happiness, and then violently abuse the admirers of Christian consistency as the dupes of deliberate duplicity.

Infidel publications abound with the most unwarrantable and reproachful epithets respecting both prophets and apostles. "The former are "strolling gentry," and the latter, if possible, incalculably worse. Our purpose is to represent these caricatures in their genuine light, by discussing as consecutively as possible a few propositions.

The subject on which the Apostles most

emphatically insisted was *Christ's resurrection.* More weight was attached to this than to any other miracle, and for many and obvious reasons. Supposing the entire truth of the Christian religion reduced to this question—

DID CHRIST ARISE FROM THE DEAD?

We now ask—*How do men present the highest possible assurance of their sincerity?* We reply

I. *By offering the utmost testimony man can give* how to ascertain if the Apostles delivered their message with that sincerity and fidelity we are permitted to expect, consider those circumstances allowed and expected to accompany truth. If you have these, then your demands on the Apostles are met, and they are true men. These circumstances are many, a few of which we will enumerate.

1. MEN SHOULD TESTIFY THAT WHICH THEY SEE.

Already have we shown the impossibility that the Apostles should have attempted deception, and it is equally manifest that they were not deluded themselves. Hundreds were witnesses of Christ's resurrection, and no proof was necessary to constitute them such save their senses. He instructed them concerning the kingdom of God for forty days, Acts i.; gave them their commission, Mark xvi.; expostulated with Peter, John xxi.; was seen of more than five hundred at once, I. Cor. 15, and lastly by Paul. They were witnesses of Him at Jerusalem, &c., Acts i. 8; see also Acts ii. 32; iii. 14, 15; v. 30–32; x. 38–41; iii. 30–31; John xx. 29. Eye witnesses are confessedly more competent than others, and here after trial, doubt and enquiry Christ is acknowledged to have risen.

Did the Apostles mistake the person of Christ?

1. The witnesses were men of competent

understanding and not likely to be cheated by palpable deceits, and probably their good sense equaled that of their calumniators. 2. They were numerous. If even a few therefore were likely to be imposed upon, it is less probable that many would. 3. The matters of fact were done in the very neighborhood where at that period they were dwelling. 4. It was not a secret occurrence. 5. The nature of the event was such as could not pass for a juggling deception. 6. The witnesses were frequently with Christ, thus rendering a delusion still less probable. 7. They were surrounded by subtle and vigilant foes, who were ever ready to assist in detecting deceits in Christ's claims.

2. MEN SHOULD TESTIFY OF THE EVENT SOON AFTER THE OCCURRENCE.

Supposing this not to have been done it is surprisingly strange that the Jews neglected to charge them with setting forth these doctrines when no one lived capable of investigating their merit. The impression was fresh on Jewish minds that Christ had been crucified. Scarcely had the rabble descended the sides of the mount, or the weeping church retired to their saddened and solitary dwellings, or the current grown cold which incarnadined Calvary's summit, when on the appointed mount in Galilee Jesus met his worshipers, and with the authority of divinity inspired holy fortitude in their bosoms by saying, "All power is given unto me in heaven and in earth." On the most solemn occasions and in the most public thoroughfares, and to immensely large multitudes of people is uttered the same thrilling sentiment. "Him hath God raised from the dead." Could they have intended to deceive?

3. WITNESSES SHOULD DELIVER THEIR TESTIMONY PLAINLY.

Addresses more pungent, pointed, plain and unmistakable in their application we question if there could be made than that on the day of Pentecost—Acts ii. 32–36. This must have been purposely to prevent mistakes. Parties purposing deception would have embodied their opinions in expressions more equivocal. But if, notwithstanding, the perspicuity prevailing in all their writings and oral instructions, it be contended there are evidences of mental reservation, equivocation, obscurity, &c., we enquire, is it not extremely unaccountable that some, amid the many of those who once were Christians of good repute, but who subsequently embraced varied heresies, and identified themselves with the Judaizers, Gnostics, Basilidians, Simonians, Ebionites, Corinthians, &c., should not have denied the truth of religion, and exposed apostolic craft. Some apostatized and embraced open infidelity; their interest and motive we might suppose would have influenced them to promulge the fraud. We find nothing of the kind, nor do we find in the sacred writings a refutation of charges of such a character.

4. THE NUMBER OF WITNESSES SHOULD BE LARGE.

A solitary few would more probably have excited suspicion. The history of the Christian Church is a history of conquests. In the face of the most formidable difficulties, it experienced the most amazing success. Its like was never before known, nor since. It was unprecedented, and without a subsequent. Of the rapidity and multiplicity of its early triumphs we possess abundant evidence in "The history of the Acts of the Apostles." In Judea where the Gospel was first preached, the new mission was most successful. On one day almost instantly following the crucifixion, three thousand persons were converted by a single sermon. A few weeks after, five thousand true believers were present in Jerusalem. Within less than ten years sequent upon Christ's death, the disciples and followers had so multiplied, particularly in and around Jerusalem, as to become objects of jealousy and alarm to ruling powers themselves. About twenty-two years after the crucifixion their number had so augmented that their name was legion. These facts may be selected from the "Acts" alone.

Nor was it among the indigent exclusively that these doctrines prevailed. They penetrated all ranks of the population. They were ardently espoused by men of exalted stations and responsible offices, whose countenancing of such a system at such a period was a most perilous adventure. Amongst those early proselytes we find Joseph of Arimathea and Nicodemus, both members of the Jewish Sanhedrim, Jairus, a ruler of the Synagogue, Zaccheus, one of the chief publicans, Apollos, a distinguished orator, Sergius, a Roman Governor of the island of Cyprus, Cornelius, a Roman Centurion, Dionysius, a judge and senator of the Athenian Areopagus, Erastus, treasurer at Corinth, Tyrannus, another Corinthian and professor of rhetoric,

Paul, learned in the Jewish law, Publius, governor of Melita, Philemon, a man of rank and influence at Colosse, Simon, a sophist of considerable note in Samaria, and Zenas, a lawyer, and even some of the Emperor's household.

Nor was the success of those principles limited to Judea. They triumphed and spread with almost incredible celerity and success through Asia Minor, Greece, Africa, and the islands of the Archipelago, and everywhere in the countries bordering on the Mediterranean. Scarcely a province of the Roman Empire but was explored by the Christian missionaries even before the demise of the Apostles. Some of its earliest and most distinguished triumphs were witnessed in the heart of Greece itself, reputed, notwithstanding the most polished nation on earth, and to whose schools and academies the aristocracy of Rome and elsewhere carried their sons to be educated for public employment. Long previous to the disappearance of the last of the twelve, churches were founded at Ephesus, Corinth, Thessalonica, Berea, Philippi and other Grecian cities. Rome, herself, the mistress of the world, and the metropolis of empire was not proof against the holy influence brought to bear. Before the close of the second century, Christians were found in almost every department of the imperial service, in the palace, the senate, the camp, and the public offices; in short everywhere, history declares, except in the temples and theaters, from which they were debarred by their holy religion.

About one hundred years following the crucifixion, lived Justin Martyr, who, speaking of the number testifying to the truth of the Gospel, says, "that there was no nation of men, whether Greeks or barbarians, not excepting those savages which wandered in clans from one region to another, and had no fixed habitation, who had not learned to offer prayers and thanksgivings to the Father and Maker of all in the name of Jesus who was crucified.

Following him, Tertullian says, "that all places but those temples (heathen) were filled with Christians, so that were they to withdraw, cities and provinces would become depopulated." So successfully was the truth propagated that Pliny declares that "he found the heathen temples in Achai almost deserted." If an individual refuses to believe this a sufficient number to testify of an event, and directly succeeding the period of its occurrence, he has sufficient obstinacy and ignorance to be an infidel.

5. WITNESSES SHOULD BE WILLING TO SUFFER FOR THEIR TESTIMONY.

The Apostles and their successors were imprisoned, racked, tortured, ridiculed, and consigned to the most torturing death, for affirming Christ's resurrection. And which of them expressed his doubt of its truth? How pertinaciously they contended they had seen him. What motive inspired them but the love of truth? What wealth did they obtain, or honor, or pleasure, or friends? What unparalleled sufferings they endured in consequence, crossing seas, traversing deserts, visiting barbarians, bearing the inclemency of almost every clime. And for what? To preach a risen Savior. Supposing them impostors how account for their remarkable conduct? How deeply in love with untruth to die for it!

ADDITIONAL CIRCUMSTANCES ACCOMPANYING TRUTH.

We might augment the number of those circumstances acknowledged universally to accompany truth. 1. If the testifier cannot anticipate any personal terrestrial advantage. 2. If his testimony tend to overthrow his worldly ease, aggrandizement, &c. 3. If the testimony of the witnesses agree. 4. If their opposers deny not that alleged, but simply attribute it to other causes. 5. If no witness either in life or death, acknowledged it a deceit. 6. If they consider and allege their salvation depending on the truth of their report. 7. If the reporters are men of various tempers, countries and civil interests. 8. If they sometimes differ, even to separation, and yet confess no falsehood in that they promulge. 9. If their testimony convince multitudes in that place and time who would have held them in contempt and abhorrence if untrue. 10. And, lastly, if they bear their testimony in such a time and place as to invite scrutiny and investigation, among enemies the most malicious, and disposed to contradict; then we consider such characters (and such were the Apostles and their immediate followers) to be most worthy of our confidence and regard.

IMPOSSIBILITY OF THE CONTRARY OF THIS.

To assert the contrary of this in the teeth of these proofs is to make the Apostles—1. To affirm a man to be God, and a deceiver the Savior of the world. 2. To frame upon untruth a new law to mankind. 3. To abuse the intellect of thousands of people with the master-piece of Satan's productions. 4. To induce tens of thousands of men and women to die martyrs for Christ, the veriest of impostors. 5. To spend their lives most unprofitably and even diabolically.

Are these things so? If the affirmative be granted, what traitors and murderers were the Apostles; of what villainy were they not guilty; what crimes did they not perpetrate. But read their lives, study their writings, and how forcibly the impossibility appears, that such numbers should so proceed, expecting no terrestrial benefit through such labors, suffering and reproach, and not a solitary man among them be constrained by conscience to detect the fraud, undeceive the world, nor even to acquaint his dearest friend on earth that the religion of Christ was the invention of man. Notwithstanding that intellectual culture of a philosophical character, of which infidels so vauntingly boast, it is obvious that their disposition is at enmity with God. A community of skeptics could not possibly exist for any considerable time. They would form society, but it would be destitute of morality, religion, a wholesome government, or a virtuous education, whilst its own principles would inevitably tend to its own disorganization. In proportion to the universality of the reception of infidelity are men disposed to injure each other, and their children disposed to follow the most demoralizing impulses. Those infernal powers incessantly on the alert to mischief mankind, are not capable of inflicting greater evils on the human race, than an infidel aristocracy of wealth, unremittingly flattering the vanity of a monarch, who, unbridling his passions, saturated with the most pernicious vices, guided by the most extravagant systems, savagely destroys his subjects without reason, and makes a merit of extermination. France and Prussia in the past are evidences of this. What morals have infidels? By what diabolical laws would they be governed? See them hurried onward in crime, sensuality and degradation, because disbelieving their accountability, because entangled in illusive theories, because sophisticated by falsehood, destitute of virtue, intoxicated in mind, and corrupt in heart. The tyrannies, the persecutions, the numberless outrages committed under the countenance of infidelity, the slavery into which it plunges the people, the reciprocal hatred and sanguinary disputes to which it has given birth, the multitudes of unhappy beings with which its demoralizing influence has filled the world, are abundantly sufficient to determine all sensible men to reject it because of its inutility, its want of consolation, its repugnance to truth. It has deluged the earth with blood, and converted the image of God into the veriest resemblance of hell.

THE APOSTLES ALSO PRESENTED DIVINE TESTIMONY.

2. But there was a testimony superhuman given by the Apostles. We now refer to the operations and miraculous endowments of the Holy Ghost. A higher testimony no one can present, and if Jehovah employed his power, was it to bewilder and deceive? Would impostors be proffered and made the receptacles of Divine influences? To reply in the affirmative is to declare that God not only permitted the deception of man in his holy name, but that he deviated from the general course of his providence purposely to secure that end. But Jew and Gentile acknowledged the reality of the miracles

wrought by the Apostles, but being repugnant to Christianity, they denied their being divinely commissioned, and asserted the influences assisting them to have originated in hell. Now, even supposing Satan capable of performing deeds (as raising the dead, &c.) transcending the unaided powers of the disciples, it is impossible to believe he would communicate his energies to a multitude of men professedly and actually counteracting his designs, impeding his Satanic progress, and seeking the overthrow of his power.

It is objected they might have surprised the people by virtue of a peculiar temperament of body. But would not the perpetual communication of their virtues to others, leave them eventually destitute themselves? Would not their poverty and privation, their sufferings, &c., destroy those virtues and render the Apostles useless?

They were Jews. Why were they exclusively possessed of this temperament? Why did none precede them? Why do none follow them?

It is further objected that a powerful imagination was of essential service. But whose imagination? What impression could the imagination of the Apostles produce on diseased persons many miles distant at the moment of healing? Was it the imagination of those on whom the miracle was wrought? But what imagination had the widow's son, the ruler's daughter, Lazarus and others? If imagination will raise the dead, it will preserve the living, and if it heal the most obstinate diseases, it is only necessary to imagine, and freedom from physical debility, and "all the ills flesh is heir to," is the instant effect.

Every truth has its proper criterion, and miracles are the evidences of the Divine commission of the Apostles. The working of miracles in support of any cause is most obviously the seal of Divinity to the truth of that cause. Those wrought by the twelve carried with them distinctive marks, distinguishing them alike from the delusions of enthusiasm and the artifices of imposture, and were appealed to with the fullest confidence of their reality and truth.

THE MIRACULOUS OPERATIONS OF THE APOSTLES.

They were many, a few of which we mention.

1. They were suddenly illumined on the descent of the Holy Spirit, and became accurately acquainted with that of which previously they were ignorant.

2. They instructed the multitudes in languages never learnt.

3. They dispossessed demoniacs of their legions, and in the name of the Crucified, tranquilized their tortured minds.

4. They raised the dead.

5. By the imposition of hands the Spirit was given to others.

6. Judgments were inflicted on delinquents by a power no less than miraculous. Ananias, Sapphira, Elymas, &c.

OBJECTIONS AND ENQUIRIES.

1. As all doctrine, Paul declares, is not from God, what do miracles attest? We reply they attest the fidelity, the veracity of him who speaks, and therefore the truthfulness of the doctrine advocated. If Paul drew a distinction between doctrines to be received and rejected, how manifestly evident his anxiety that fraud should be detected and exposed. We consider the conservation of Christianity amidst the most unparalleled sufferings, one of the most astounding and satisfactory miraculous operations ever witnessed or reported. I will not trouble you with a description of the Ten Persecutions, but in the annals of Tacitus we perceive the Christians were held in utter detestation. He describes them as believers in a "deplo-

rable and destructive superstition," and then as if wanting a name to give them, adds—*vulgus Christianos appellabat*—the vulgar people call them. Christians. This historian writes of them with an air of contempt. But, however, their exterior towards them soon became changed. From a handful of obscure and unnoticeable men they grew into a gigantic community, having their missionaries and organizations throughout every corner of the Roman Empire. It was then their persecutions began to assume those shapes and proportions necessary to attract history. Then the Pagan priests, Pagan magistrates and aristocracy, commenced earnestly to check the tendencies of the "sect every where spoken against," and to rouse and infuriate the superstitious prejudices and passions of the populace against the innovators. And this was speedily done, for one reason probably among others, that Christianity increasingly proselytizing was singularly exclusive.

It denied and rejected every alleged fact and article of heathen mythology. It heard no compromise, no amalgamation, and was content to prevail only by the subversion of every altar, statue and temple consecrated to pagan uses. All other gods were pronounced false, and all other worship an abomination. It was then impossible to escape persecution from the pagan rabble or superstitious priesthood. The priests trembled for their revenues, the rulers for their power, the rich for their wealth and station, a spiritual equality among all ranks was proclaimed. Persecutions multiplied but were unsuccessful. The most public Christians were accused of crimes the most atrocious and revolting. They were condemned to a variety of deaths, and perished amidst all manners of insults and execrations. Some were sewed up in the skins of wild beasts and then thrown to be devoured by dogs. Some, like their divine Master, were nailed to crosses, others were wrapped in pitched clothing; these were set on fire, and being lighted up at night served as torches to illumine Nero's gardens. These barbarities were followed by edicts enjoining upon the authorities to repress the new religion by every means placed at their disposal by the law. Many martyrs were in consequence. But in despite of injustice, intolerance and abhorrence Christianity, upheld by omnipotence and directed by infinite intelligence, mightily prevailed.

QUESTION—WHY ARE NOT MIRACLES CONTINUED ?

I. We have the full use and benefit of the Holy Ghost so abundantly then bestowed, when miracles prevailed. The seal originally placed to the Scriptures has never been removed. Must God work miracles before every man and in every age, or be rejected? What if all Christ's works have been done in Washington, and all had seen them but one man, must none believe but those that saw. Should no man believe that there have been wars in America but those who saw the battles? or what if those things had been done in our forefathers' days, should we not have believed them, except they had been done in ours? We have as full testimony of Christ's and his Apostles' works, as we can have of any of these.

2. The Holy Spirit is still continued to every member of the Church, though not precisely to the same use.

3. The promise is fulfilled if it can be shown that these signs (Mark xvi. 17) followed in the case of any that believed, and it is not necessary to suppose they would follow in the case of all. The infidel cannot say that the promise has not been fulfilled, unless he can show that these events never occurred. Miracles were necessary for the establishment of religion in the world; they are not necessary now.

4. That doctrine could not possibly be divine that would declare it necessary that God should satisfy every unreasonable infidel by miracles. Ordinary human testimony is sufficient to inform us of the certainty of former miracles, and those miracles are sufficient attestation on God's part of his acknowledging the doctrine so attested. Punishment rather than satisfaction would be the desert of him refusing to believe until he could see, for on such terms if all people but one were witnesses of any miraculous act, it must be repeated for his conviction by reason of his obstinacy. Providential government would then be destroyed.

5. We are to infer their non-necessity from their non-repetition. If rational conviction can be attributed to the sight of miracles exclusively, miracles would never have been withdrawn.

6. But thousands are being unceasingly convinced of the divinity of the Christian

religion without the renewing of miracles, their presence then is not of absolute necessity.

It is alleged that persons professedly convinced are deluded frequently—We reply

1. The Apostles, to both their utmost happiness and our satisfaction, assure us in regard to themselves of the contrary. 2. And they were ever ready to demonstrate the ignorance of their questioners. 3. We are instructed not to believe all wonders which may occur. Things hostile to natural religion or revealed religion confirmed by miracles, most unquestionably are to be rejected. If God has once convinced the understanding, it is obligatory on man to cherish the light thus imparted. Satan, too, attempted the imitation of Christ, but as a statue may be distinguished from the Creator, so may Satanic fictions from divine realities.

HOW ASCERTAIN THE TRUTH OF MIRACLES.

1. You should understand miracles were predicted hundreds of years before they were wrought. 2. The doctrine delivered bears God's image, and was confirmed in the name of Christ. Impostors do not realize divine assistance. 3. If deceivers attempt the accomplishment of that transcending their abilities, they inevitably experience defeat and mortification. A miracle was demanded from Mahomet but when did he ever seriously attempt the gratification of his followers? Maimon in a letter to French Jews relates of one El David who pretended himself Christ, a circumstance illustrative of my idea. This impostor was brought before an Arabian prince, who asked him, what miracle he showed to merit belief? He answered, "Cut off my head and I will live again." "Thou canst give us no greater sign," replied the prince, "and if it so fall out that thou dost

rise again to life, after I have cut off thy head I and my people, nay, all the world, sure, will believe what thou sayest is true." The experiment was made—you believe the result. Discover one failure in the Apostles because of imposition and you render them obnoxious, to indignation and contempt. 4. There were no symptoms of enthusiasm displayed by the Apostles other than the most fastidious minds might be enabled to countenance. Their intellects were clear and calm. There appēared no unusual preparation, and natural inclination toward the undertaking in which they enlisted. They rather exhibited prejudice to the main articles of their faith, the death and resurrection of Christ, and in them hope seems to have died, when their Master gave up the ghost.—*An objection that promises were not fulfilled.*—Mark x. 29, 30.

This is a specimen of that class of unfulfilled promises. That man who fails to perceive the meaning of this to be such an earthly recompense as is consistent with persecution is not too enlightened to be an infidel. Besides this promise cannot refer to earthly possessions but in a very inferior degree. External accommodation is invariably estimated secondary to religious joy by the wise and good. The pardon of sin, God's favor, quietude of conscience, consolation in death. Parents, &c., spiritually these most fully fulfill the promise, and most agreeably to the Apostles' anticipations and desires.

THE BIBLE OBSCURE.

It is said some portions of holy writ are too obscure to allow any reasonable explication. But is its obscurity an argument against its divinity? Every science may be objected to by the uninitiated for the same reason, if reason it be. Is all to be rejected, because some is incomprehensible? How perspicuous is the plan of salvation to the spirit-taught heart. Those portions transcending the grasp of the intellect are revealed as objects of faith more than of understanding. Unbeliever, do you not comprehend sufficient to condemn you?

CONTRADICTIONS.

Enemies say there are irreconcilable differences in the Scripture.

1. This may appear a fact to the unreflecting and prejudiced, for they find contradictions in every system. The revolution of the earth was to the pope and cardinals, and is to thousands now. Are those writings impugning the Scriptures without contradictions? The Scriptures in very early days were venerated and ardently studied and expounded by men in contrast with whom modern skeptics are a race of dwarfs. Objections now originate in ignorance or prejudice. 2. But wherein do those contradictions appear? Do they concern the minor circumstances of religion, as time, place, &c., and

allow those portions true on which my salvation depends? The very apparent want of agreement inspires me with fresh confidence in their authenticity. Men deliberately deceptive would have exercised more caution to prevent suspicion than the Bible writers appear to have displayed. 3. But consider the manner in which objections have been repeatedly refuted. If one portion of the inspired writings appears less confirmed or more exposed to the charge of contradiction than another, that is selected as having charms for cavilers of which others are destitute. How manifestly lacking of both judgment and candor. Have you naturally considered the difficulty now encountered in understanding accurately the ground of chronology? There may be errors in chronology and computations, but in all such difficulties we should make the greatest allowances. Transcribers may have unintentionally committed blunders in dates and localities, but not in doctrines is it so probable. They were not inspired to copy as the Apostles were to write and speak. Allowances for interregnums, customs of genealogies, &c., present even the Jews with puzzles, but they repudiate not the Old Testament on that account: No improbability can be shown in the accounts transmitted to us, and no sufficient reason therefore can be drawn to denounce as a fiction the holiest and most useful book extant. Protracted study disabuses the mind, and shows that to possess the utmost transparency which was previously contemned as ambiguous and contradictory.

SCRIPTURE BOTH GENERALLY AND PARTICULARLY TRUE.

What may be asserted concerning the truth of Scripture generally, holds equally valid when applied particularly.

1. If the Bible is proved true, then those apparently contradictory passages are true

also. Men are frequently ashamed of their unprovoked rashness in censuring the inspired volume when persons of intelligence have manifested to them their ignorance of the plainest doctrinal truths.

2. The most improbable passages are equally true,—as the sun standing still, the fall of Jericho's walls—Christ walking on the sea, &c.

3. And likewise those portions denouncing vengeance on unbelievers.

CLOSE.

If sufficient has not been written to convert you, unbelieving reader, from the error of your ways, it may have convinced you of those numerous and weighty obligations under which you exist to both God and man. In answering enquiries and overturning objections, we have aimed at presenting reasons for our belief. Your tastes I have not contemplated, your religious interests I have. Suppose not because you profess sincerity in your errors, your guilt is extinguished. Good intentions will not justify blasphemy, nor infuse sanctity into outrage and murder.

If sincerity sanctifies immorality, in one country Christianity may be lauded, and in another cursed, and thus impudence and inspiration be made to utter the same language.

Remember, it is easier to asperse truth than to refute or practice it. I have not assaulted your judgment with naked fallacy, but truth. I would hope it is too evident to be overlooked, and too strong to be overcome. Are you determined to live in infidelity as if future terrors were only terrific dreams, or mere productions of a feverish and disordered brain? The practice of religion here is necessary to happiness hereafter. Search after truth with serenity and candor. Despise not religion and sobriety. But should Christianity be contrary to your professed anticipations and belief, then must you bid farewell to life and pleasure together. Your last breath extinguishes joy, and kindles a flame to torment rather than consume. Your music ends in tears, your pleasure in unavailing repentance, your repentance in despair.

How doleful the catastrophe to be dragged from your domicile to a dungeon, and from the embraces of affectionate friends to those of everlasting flames. To my youthful readers, especially, I would say dangers surround you and perhaps unseen and disregarded. Temptations assail you, not with the violence of a foe but the caresses of a friend, and eventually you may surrender to temptation without presenting a solitary attempt at resistance. Oh, why are immortal spirits tied to all the infamous impressions of flesh and blood! Men appear to bind themselves vassals to Satan for pleasure in possession and torments in reversion.

Infidelity and Christianity, then, are before you. Choose which you will serve. The one invites you to love God and your kind, to preserve your existence, and augment the sum of human happiness; the other to love only formidable evil, detest joy, renounce the most pleasing sensations, the most legitimate pleasures of the heart. Christianity counsels you to consult the Bible, and adopt it as your guide; infidelity portrays Revelation as a treacherous director, infallibly conducting you astray. Christianity urges on you real enlightenment, the importance of truth; infidelity enjoins a career tending to cloud the understanding, to remain ignorant of spiritual truth, to believe no relations so important to your interests as those subsisting between yourselves and pursuits obviously subversive of all happiness. Christianity instructs you to moderate your desires, to resist them when found obstructive to moral progress, to counteract them by motives inculcated by Revelation; infidelity enjoins you to cherish evil, and to combat your propensities with motives which, in fact, facilitate their exercise and augment their power. Christianity exhorts man to strengthen the social principle it has implanted, to love his fellows, to be peaceable, benevolent, liberal; infidelity admonishes you to secure immoral society, flee the associations of the pious, dissolve the most sacred bonds, torment and injure those not conforming to your views. Christianity would have you be courageous, industrious, cultivate the domestic affections, consecrate your influence to God, improve human society, blush for your vices, repent and believe in Christ; infidelity would have you extol the profligate who has disturbed public tranquillity, prefer iniquity to piety, scatter with lavish hand the seeds of discord, promote the carnage of your fellow creatures, haughtily despise Heaven's grace, saying, "live and die like a philosopher." My dear readers, take those truths into your most secret and sacred retirement. Identify yourselves with God's people. Renounce connection with the foes of truth, and be encouraged to embrace religion by the gracious expression of our dear Redeemer—HIM THAT COMETH UNTO ME, I WILL IN NO WISE CAST OUT.

www.ingramcontent.com/pod-product-compliance
Lightning Source LLC
LaVergne TN
LVHW021424110826
845150LV00007B/2073